MANGA DRAWING

WITH PEGASUS, GRIFFINS, AND OTHER WINGED BEASTS

written by Naomi Hughes
illustrated by Ludovic Sallé

CAPSTONE PRESS
a capstone imprint

Published by Capstone Press, an imprint of Capstone
1710 Roe Crest Drive, North Mankato, Minnesota 56003
capstonepub.com

Copyright © 2026 by Capstone. All rights reserved. No part of this publication may be reproduced in whole or in part, or stored in a retrieval system, or transmitted in any form or by any means, electronic, mechanical, photocopying, recording, or otherwise, without written permission of the publisher.

Cataloging-in-Publication Data is available on the Library of Congress website.

ISBN: 9798875221613 (hardcover)
ISBN: 9798875221576 (ebook PDF)

Summary: Following illustrated step-by-step instructions, artists of all abilities can learn how to draw Pegasus, griffins, and more winged beasts of myth in the dynamic manga art style.

Editorial Credits
Editor: Abby Cich; Designer: Hilary Wacholz; Production Specialist: Tori Abraham

Any additional websites and resources referenced in this book are not maintained, authorized, or sponsored by Capstone. All product and company names are trademarks™ or registered® trademarks of their respective holders.

The publisher and the author shall not be liable for any damages allegedly arising from the information in this book, and they specifically disclaim any liability from the use or application of any of the contents of this book.

Printed and bound in the USA. 006307

TABLE OF CONTENTS

Fantastic Fliers 4

Supplies 5

Pegasus 6

Phoenix 8

Griffin 10

Tengu 12

Dragon 14

Adze 16

Harpy 18

Mothman 20

Impundulu 22

Pixie 24

Sphinx 26

Fire and Lightning 28

Draw More Manga Creatures! 32

About the Author 32

About the Illustrator 32

FANTASTIC FLIERS

When you think of wings, what do you picture?

Maybe it's tiny, gleaming pixie wings. Or blazing phoenix feathers. Many myths feature amazing flying creatures like these. Now, you can learn to draw them in an awesome style—manga!

Manga is a lot like comics. It tells a story using art. Manga got its start in Japan. But today, it's popular all over the world. From cute animal stories to epic adventures, manga's got tales for everyone.

Manga art has its own style. Artists draw characters in poses full of action and emotion. They can also use special symbols to show mood. Human characters often have large, shiny eyes and small mouths. Don't forget neat hairstyles! Giant hair spikes, bright colors, and more show off spunky personalities. Manga creatures show off, too, with over-the-top features. Cute critters might have big, round faces and sparkly eyes. Monsters are often drawn with lots of angles, like pointy chins and sharp teeth.

Manga is perfect for drawing your favorite legendary fliers! And it's time to try it for yourself.

Get ready to draw Pegasus, griffins, and other winged beasts . . . MANGA STYLE!

SUPPLIES

Paper. Plain copy paper works well, but many artists use sketch paper.

Pencil. Keep the point sharp (or use a mechanical pencil) and draw lightly. That way, you can easily erase when you need.

Eraser. Because no one draws perfectly all of the time! Plus, manga drawings may take extra practice. Test your eraser first to make sure it doesn't smudge or tear the paper.

Pen. Use a black marker pen with a fine tip or a regular pen. Once you're done with your pencil sketch, trace over it with pen. This will make the lines in your art dark and bold.

Colored markers, colored pencils, or crayons. If you'd like, add color to your art after you've outlined it in pen. Check the ink is dry first so your lines stay crisp.

DID YOU KNOW?
Pro manga artists have special dip pens and ink pots. They use these tools to draw the lines in their final art.

PEGASUS

Horses may gallop across the land. But this one can soar across the sky! Pegasus originally lived in Greece. The mighty winged steed carried heroes into battle. Its actions were so epic that humans named a constellation after it. Now, Pegasus is always among the stars.

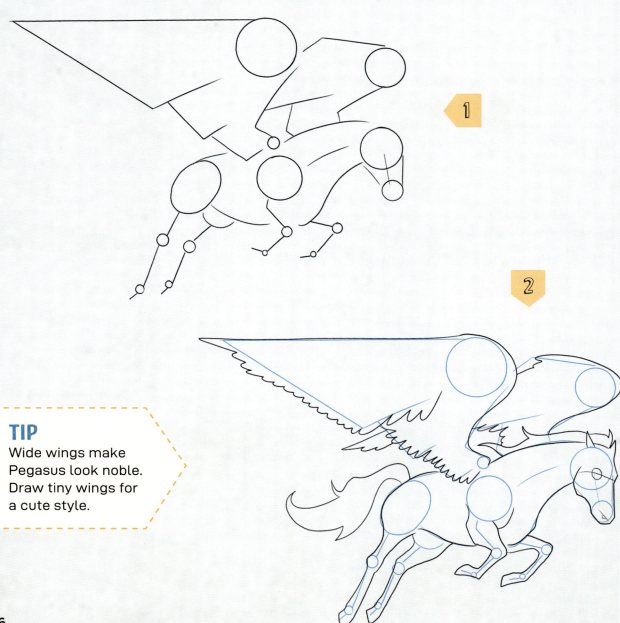

TIP
Wide wings make Pegasus look noble. Draw tiny wings for a cute style.

PHOENIX

How long does a phoenix live? Some legends say it never truly dies! Instead, these regal birds burn up in flames. Then, they are reborn from the ashes. Phoenixes were first sighted long ago in Egypt, Greece, and Rome. Today, people all over the world tell tales of these fiery fowl.

TIP
A phoenix can be many colors! Try ember red, blazing yellow, rusty orange, or a mix.

GRIFFIN

Talk about a menacing mash-up! Griffins glide through the air with strong eagle wings. They prowl on land with powerful lion bodies. Between their sharp cat claws and hooked bird beak, prey doesn't stand a chance! These fierce predators were first sighted ages ago. Since then, they've been seen hunting in Asia, Greece, and beyond.

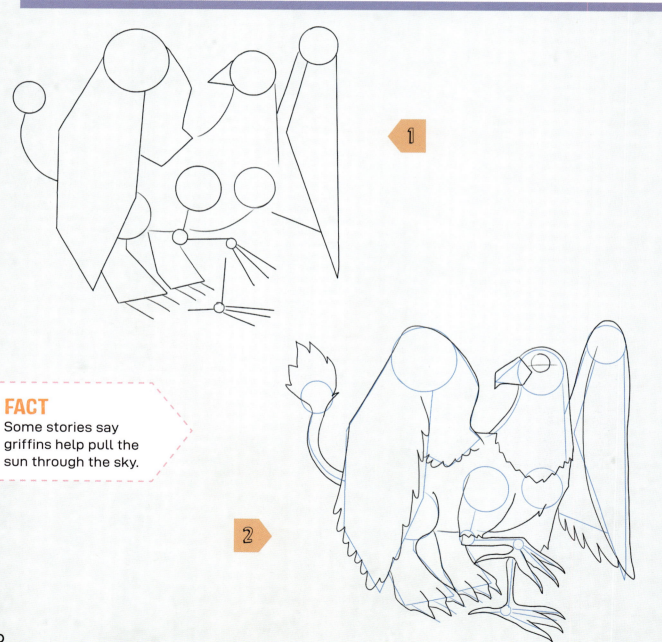

FACT
Some stories say griffins help pull the sun through the sky.

TENGU

Never get in a fight with a tengu! These part-bird, part-human creatures are masters of war. They use swords to defend their mountain homes. Some people seek tengu out to learn their sword skills. Others fear these strong beings. Either way, their bright red skin and long noses make them easy to spot.

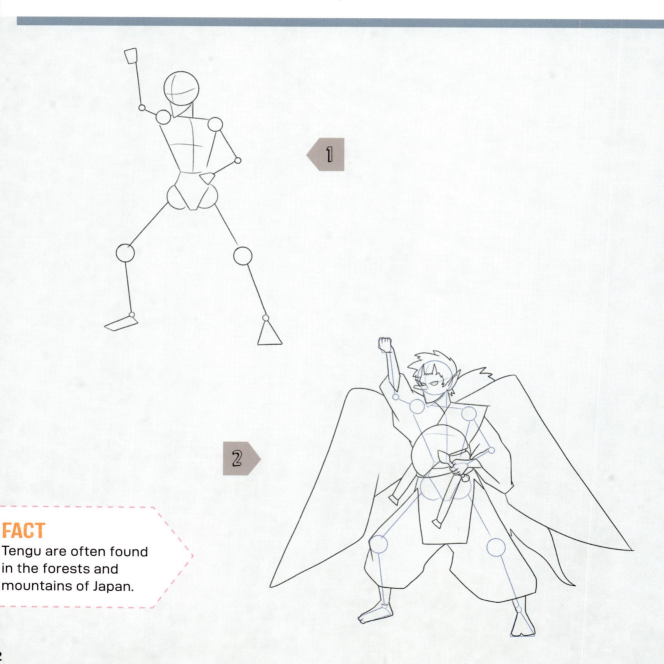

FACT
Tengu are often found in the forests and mountains of Japan.

DRAGON

These scaly monsters come in many sizes. Most are large. Some can grow as big as hills! Their incredible strength makes them tough to take down. So do their sharp claws and teeth, powerful wings, and fiery breath. If a dragon decides to make trouble, look out!

1

TIP
Dragons have unique traits. Try different types of horns, or more spikes on the wings.

2

14

ADZE

Does this creature look like a firefly? It's a trick! It's really an adze. These creepy South African critters can change shape. Sometimes they're human. Other times, they're fireflies. As bugs, they slip through windows and door cracks. Once they're inside, they sneak up on sleeping people to sip their blood.

TIP
Around the adze are impact lines. In manga, these lines show that something is startling, loud, or moving fast.

HARPY

Most people think harpies are ugly. But they weren't always that way. At first, these birdlike beings were graceful wind spirits. They traveled in storms. They ran errands for greater spirits. Then later, harpies became cruel, ugly, and stinky. The creatures even used their awful smell as a weapon! Why did they change? We may never know.

FACT
Harpies are ancient. They were first spotted over 2,000 years ago.

18

MOTHMAN

Mothman is a seriously spooky specimen. His glowing red eyes pierce the dark. His giant moth wings carry him through the night. He was spotted in 1967 in West Virginia right before a large bridge collapsed. Did he cause it? No one knows. One thing is for sure: Mothman is one of the United States' most unsettling legends.

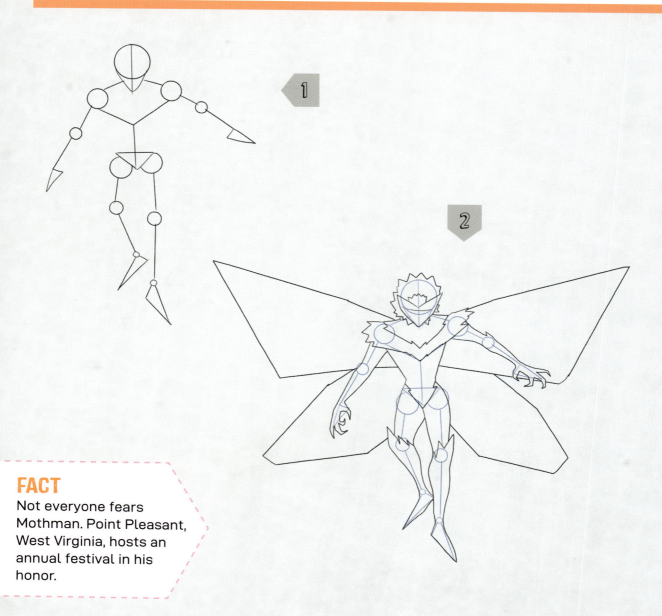

FACT
Not everyone fears Mothman. Point Pleasant, West Virginia, hosts an annual festival in his honor.

IMPUNDULU

With a flap of its wings, this special bird creates lightning! Booms of thunder echo across the sky wherever it flies. But it has a habit even spookier than making storms. It's rumored to drink blood. This animal is usually spotted in South Africa. When you see a flash in the clouds, keep an eye out for the impundulu.

TIP
Add dark storm clouds for a spooky background.

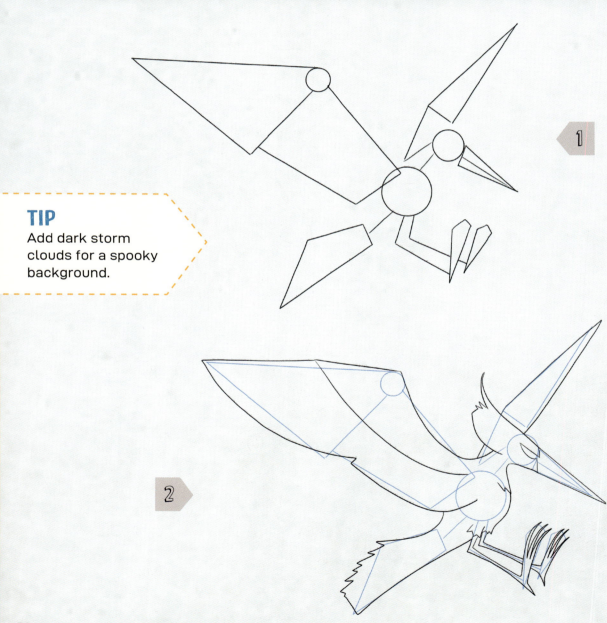

PIXIE

From a safe distance, pixies look cute. They like to dance and play in puddles. But be careful. These tiny creatures can cause big trouble. They like to scare people and play tricks. One of their favorite pranks is leading travelers astray. If you spot a pixie in the woods, don't follow it!

TIP
In manga, pointy teeth are often used to make a character feel sneaky, but still playful and cute.

24

SPHINX

Sphinxes are famous for their wisdom. They love to test people with puzzles and riddles. If you answer incorrectly, watch out! They might just eat you. That was what one sphinx did a long time ago. A Greek hero stopped that beast. But others are still out there. Better brush up on your puzzle-solving skills!

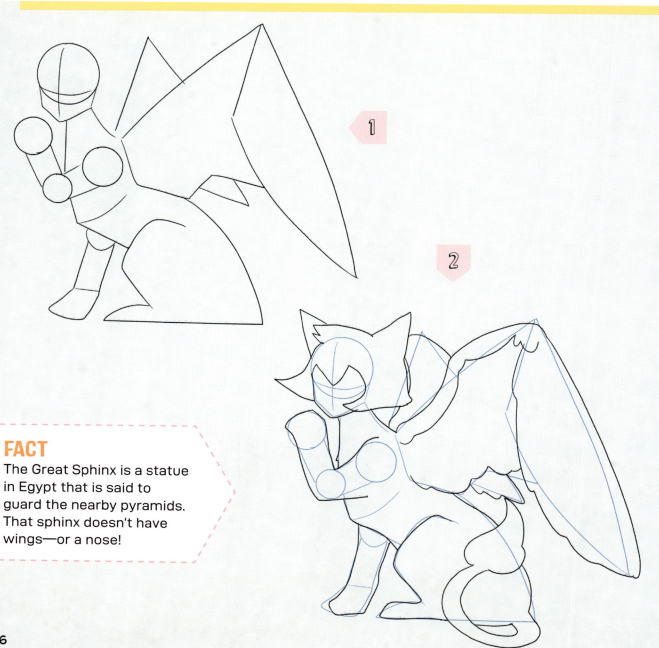

FACT
The Great Sphinx is a statue in Egypt that is said to guard the nearby pyramids. That sphinx doesn't have wings—or a nose!

FIRE AND LIGHTNING

The sky is alive with energy as two majestic birds circle each other. Flames blaze from the phoenix's trailing feathers. Lightning flashes from the impundulu's great wings. Do you think they're dancing? Or playing a game? Either way, these fancy fliers are putting on a beautiful show.

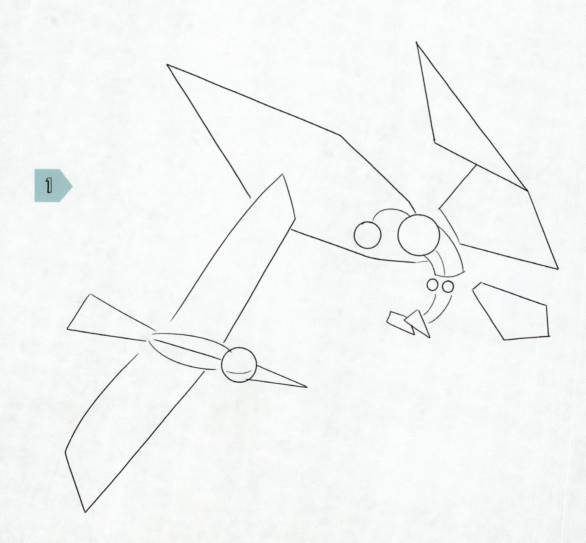

1

4

TIP
See how these birds form a circle? Creating a shape with characters like this can help your art feel complete.

30

5

DRAW MORE MANGA CREATURES!

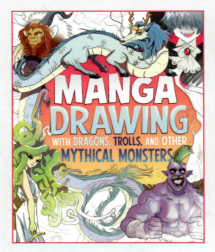
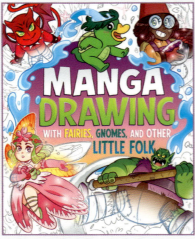
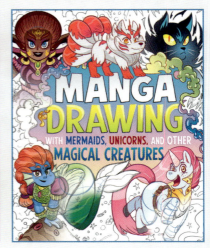

ABOUT THE AUTHOR

Naomi Hughes is an author and school librarian in Minnesota, where she lives with her family and a house full of pets. She writes all sorts of books for kids, from nonfiction picture books to science fiction and fantasy for teens. She loves all things manga and anime and also enjoys traveling, reading, escape games, and going on adventures.

ABOUT THE ILLUSTRATOR

Ludovic Sallé is a French artist who enjoys working both traditionally with watercolor and acrylic, as well as digitally. His manga-inspired style allows him to explore a dynamic, colorful graphic universe and to create cute characters.